In the Year 1980

by

Kerry Butters.

In the Year 1980.

Millennium: 2nd millennium

Centuries: 19th century – **20th century** – 21st century

Decades: 1950s 1960s 1970s – **1980s** – 1990s 2000s 2010s

Years: 1977 1978 1979 – **1980** – 1981 1982 1983

1980 (MCMLXXX) was a leap year starting on Tuesday
(dominical letter FE) of the Gregorian calendar, the 1980th year of
the Common Era (CE) and *Anno Domini* (AD) designations, the
980th year of the 2nd millennium, the 80th year of the
20th century, and the 1st year of the 1980s decade.

Contents

Events

January

- January 1 – Changes to the Swedish Act of Succession make Princess Victoria of Sweden first in line to the throne ("heir apparent") and therefore Crown Princess, ahead of her younger brother.
- January 4 – U.S. President Jimmy Carter proclaims a grain embargo against the USSR with the support of the European Commission.
- January 6
  - Global Positioning System time epoch begins at 00:00 UTC.
  - The president of Sicily, Piersanti Mattarella, is killed by the Mafia.
- January 9 – In Saudi Arabia, 63 Islamist insurgents are beheaded for their part in the siege of the Great Mosque in Mecca in November, 1979.
- January 11 – Nigel Short, 14, becomes the youngest chess player to be awarded the degree of International Master.

- January 20 – Cuba recognizes the Sahrawi Arab Democratic Republic (SADR).
- January 21
  - The London Gold Fixing hits its highest price ever (adjusted for inflation), at US$850 a troy ounce.
  - MS *Athina B* is beached at Brighton, becoming a temporary tourist attraction.
  - At least 200 people are killed when the Corralejas Bullring collapses at Sincelejo, Colombia.
- January 22 – Andrei Sakharov, Soviet scientist and human rights activist, is arrested in Moscow.
- January 24 – The Chicago, Rock Island and Pacific Railroad is ordered liquidated due to bankruptcy, and debt owed to creditors.
- January 26 – Israel and Egypt establish diplomatic relations.
- January 27 – Canadian Caper: Six United States diplomats, posing as Canadians, manage to escape from Tehran, Iran as they board a flight to Zürich, Switzerland on Swissair.
- January 31 – The Spanish Embassy in Guatemala is invaded and set on fire, killing 36 people. It is called "Spain's own Tehran", similar to the 1979–80 Iran American hostage crisis.

February

- February 2 – Abscam: FBI personnel target members of the Congress of the United States in a sting operation.
- February 2–3 – The New Mexico State Penitentiary riot takes place; 33 inmates are killed and more than 100 inmates injured.

- February 4 – Ayatollah Ruhollah Khomeini names Abolhassan Banisadr as president of Iran.
- February 13 – The 1980 Winter Olympics open in Lake Placid, New York.
- February 15 – In Vanuatu, followers of John Frum's cargo cult on the island of Tanna declare secession as the nation of Tafea.
- February 16 – A total solar eclipse is seen in North Africa and West Asia.
- February 22 – The United States Olympic Hockey Team defeats the Soviet Union in the semifinals of the Winter Olympics, in the *Miracle on Ice*.
- February 23 – Ayatollah Ruhollah Khomeini states that Iran's parliament will decide the fate of the American embassy hostages.
- February 25 – A coup in Suriname ousts the government of Henck Arron; leaders Dési Bouterse and Roy Horb replace it with a National Military Council.
- February 27
  - M-19 guerrillas begin the Dominican embassy siege in Colombia, holding 60 people hostage, including 14 ambassadors.
  - Iran recognizes the Sahrawi Arab Democratic Republic (SADR).

March

- March 1
  - The Commonwealth Trade Union Council is established.

- The *Voyager 1* probe confirms the existence of Janus, a moon of Saturn.
- March 3
  - Pierre Trudeau returns to office as Prime Minister of Canada.
  - The Audi Quattro, a four-wheel drive sporting coupe, is launched in West Germany.
- March 4 – Robert Mugabe is elected Prime Minister of Zimbabwe.
- March 8 – The Soviet Union's first rock music festival starts.
- March 14 – LOT Polish Airlines Flight 007 crashes during an emergency landing near Warsaw, Poland, killing a 14-man American boxing team and 73 others.
- March 18 – Fifty people are killed at the Plesetsk Cosmodrome in Russia, when a Vostok-2M rocket explodes on its launch pad during a fueling operation.
- March 19–20 – The MV *Mi Amigo*, the ship housing pirate radio station Radio Caroline, sinks off the English coast (the station returns aboard a new ship in 1983).
- March 21
  - U.S. President Jimmy Carter announces that the United States will boycott the 1980 Summer Olympics in Moscow.
  - *Mafioso* Angelo Bruno is murdered in Philadelphia.
- March 22 – The Georgia Guidestones are erected in Elbert County, Georgia.
- March 24
  - The Australia Olympic Committee announces it will send an Olympic delegation to Moscow, despite objections by Prime Minister Malcolm Fraser.

- ○ Archbishop Óscar Romero is killed by gunmen while celebrating Mass in San Salvador.
- March 26 – A mine lift cage at the Vaal Reefs gold mine in South Africa falls 1.2 miles (1.9 kilometers), killing 23.
- March 27
  - ○ The Norwegian oil platform Alexander L. Kielland collapses in the North Sea, killing 123 of its crew of 212.
  - ○ The Silver Thursday market crash occurs.
  - ○ Sierra Leone recognizes the Sahrawi Arab Democratic Republic (SADR).
- March 28 – Talpiot Tomb is found in Jerusalem.
- March 31 – Chicago, Rock Island and Pacific Railroad operates its final train.

April

- April 1
  - ○ The Southern African Development Coordination Conference (SADCC) is formed in Lusaka, Zambia.
  - ○ The Mariel boatlift from Cuba begins.
  - ○ New York City's Transport Works Union Local 100 goes on strike, which continues for 11 days.
  - ○ The 1980 United States Census begins. There are 226,545,805 United States residents on this day.
- April 2 – The St Pauls riot breaks out in Bristol.
- April 7 – The United States severs diplomatic relations with Iran and imposes economic sanctions, following the taking of American hostages on November 4, 1979.

- April 10 – In Lisbon, Portugal, the governments of Spain and the United Kingdom agree to reopen the border between Gibraltar and Spain in 1985, closed since 1969.
- April 12
  - Samuel Kanyon Doe takes over Liberia in a *coup d'état*, ending over 130 years of democratic presidential succession in that country.
  - Terry Fox begins his Marathon of Hope from St. Johns, Newfoundland, Canada.
- April 14 – Iron Maiden's debut self-titled album *Iron Maiden* is released.
- April 15 – Libya and Syria recognize the Sahrawi Arab Democratic Republic (SADR).
- April 18 – Zimbabwe gains de jure independence from the United Kingdom; Robert Mugabe becomes Prime Minister.
- April 21 – Rosie Ruiz wins the Boston Marathon, but is later exposed as a fraud and stripped of her award.
- April 24 – Pennsylvania Lottery Scandal: the Pennsylvania Lottery is rigged by 6 men including the host of the live TV drawing, Nick Perry.
- April 24–25 – Operation Eagle Claw, a commando mission in Iran to rescue American embassy hostages, is aborted after mechanical problems ground the rescue helicopters. Eight United States troops are killed in a mid-air collision during the failed operation.
- April 25 – Dan-Air Flight 1008 crashes in Tenerife, killing all 146 occupants and marking the worst air disaster involving a British-registered aircraft in terms of loss of life.
- April 26 – Louise and Charmian Faulkner disappear from outside their flat in St Kilda, Victoria, Australia.

- April 27 – The Dominican embassy siege ends with all hostages released and the guerrillas flying to Cuba.
- April 28 – Swaziland recognizes the Sahrawi Arab Democratic Republic (SADR).
- April 30
  - Iranian Embassy siege: Six Iranian-born terrorists take over the Iranian embassy in London, UK. SAS retakes the Embassy on May 5; 1 terrorist survives.
  - Queen Juliana of the Netherlands abdicates, and her daughter Beatrix accedes to the throne.

May

- May 2 – Referendum on system of government held in Nepal.
- May 4 – Yugoslav President Josip Broz Tito dies. The funeral ceremony later becomes a large diplomatic meeting and media event, with more than 140 state delegations in Belgrade from all over the world (only the funeral of Pope John Paul II in April 2005 will have more news coverage and a higher number of delegations).
- May 7 – Paul Geidel, convicted of second-degree murder in 1911, is released from prison in Beacon, New York, after 68 years and 245 days (the longest-ever time served by an inmate).
- May 8 – Global eradication of smallpox endorsed by the World Health Assembly
- May 9
  - In Florida, the Liberian freighter *Summit Venture* hits the Sunshine Skyway Bridge over Tampa Bay. A 1,400-

foot section of the bridge collapses and 35 people (most in a bus) are killed.
- o The Norco shootout takes place in California.
- o James Alexander George Smith "Jags" McCartney the Turks and Caicos Islands' first Chief Minister, is killed in a plane crash over New Jersey.
- May 11 – Mobster Henry Hill is arrested for drug possession.
- May 14 – Botswana recognizes the Sahrawi Arab Democratic Republic (SADR).
- May 17
  - o A Tampa, Florida court acquits 4 white police officers of killing Arthur McDuffie, a black insurance executive, provoking 3 days of race riots in Miami.
  - o Internal conflict in Peru: On the eve of presidential elections, Maoist guerrilla group Shining Path attacks a polling location in the town of Chuschi, Ayacucho.
- May 18
  - o The 1980 eruption of Mount St. Helens kills 57 and causes US$3 billion in damage.
  - o Ian Curtis, singer/songwriter of acclaimed post-punk band Joy Division, is found hanged.
- May 18 –27 – Gwangju Uprising: Students in Gwangju, South Korea begin demonstrations, calling for democratic reforms.
- May 20 – 1980 Quebec referendum: Voters in Quebec reject by a vote of 60% a proposal to seek independence from Canada.
- May 21 – *The Empire Strikes Back* is released.
- May 22 – Pac-Man (the best-selling arcade game of all time) is released in Japan.

- May 24
  - The International Court of Justice calls for the release of U.S. Embassy hostages in Tehran.
  - The New York Islanders win their first Stanley Cup, from a goal by Bobby Nystrom in game six overtime of the 1980 Stanley Cup Finals over the Philadelphia Flyers.
- May 25 – Indianapolis 500: Johnny Rutherford wins for a third time in car owner Jim Hall's revolutionary ground effect Chaparral car; the victory is Hall's second as an owner.
- May 26
  - John Frum supporters in Vanuatu storm government offices on the island of Tanna. Vanuatu government troops land the next day and drive them away.
  - In South Korea, military government forces and pro-democracy protesters clash; 2,000 protesters die.
  - Vernon Jordan is shot and critically injured in an assassination attempt in Fort Wayne, Indiana by Joseph Paul Franklin (the first major news story for CNN).
- May 28 – A fiery bus crash near the small village of Webb, Saskatchewan claims 22 lives.

June

- June 1 – The first 24-hour news channel Cable News Network (CNN) is launched.
- June 3 – A series of deadly tornadoes strikes Grand Island, Nebraska, causing over $300m in damage, killing 5 people and injuring over 250.

- June 9 – In Los Angeles, comedian Richard Pryor is badly burned trying to freebase cocaine.
- June 10
    - Apartheid: The African National Congress in South Africa publishes a statement by their imprisoned leader Nelson Mandela.
    - A Unabomber bomb injures United Airlines president Percy Wood in Lake Forest, Illinois.
- June 20 – Augusta AVA becomes the first federally recognized American Viticultural Area.
- June 23 – September 6 – The 1980 United States heat wave claims 1,700 lives.
- June 23 – Tim Berners-Lee begins work on ENQUIRE, the system that will eventually lead to the creation of the World Wide Web in fall of 1990.
- June 25 – A Muslim Brotherhood assassination attempt against Syrian president Hafez al-Assad fails. Assad retaliates by sending the army against them.
- June 26 – Aerolinee Itavia Flight 870 crashes into the sea near Palermo after an explosion occurs in the air; 81 people die. A bomb or a missile is suspected to be the cause of the accident but no culprits are ever found.
- June 27 – U.S. President Jimmy Carter signs Proclamation 4771, requiring 18- to 25-year-old males to register for a peacetime military draft, in response to the Soviet invasion of Afghanistan.
- June 29 – Vigdís Finnbogadóttir is elected President of Iceland making her the first woman democratically elected as head of state.

July

July 10: Fire at Alexandra Palace.

- July 4 – Chad and Mali recognize the Sahrawi Arab Democratic Republic (SADR).
- July 8 – A wave of strikes begins in Lublin, Poland.
- July 9
  - Pope John Paul II visits Brazil; 7 people are crushed to death in a crowd meeting him.
  - Zimbabwe recognizes the Sahrawi Arab Democratic Republic (SADR).
- July 15 – A severe and destructive thunderstorm strikes 4 counties in western Wisconsin, including the city of Eau Claire. It causes over $250m in damage, and 1 person is killed.
- July 16 – Former California Governor and actor Ronald Reagan is nominated for U.S. President, at the 1980 Republican National Convention in Detroit. Influenced by the Religious Right, the convention also drops its long standing support for the Equal Rights Amendment, dismaying moderate Republicans.
- July 19 – Former Turkish Prime Minister Nihat Erim is killed by 2 gunmen in Istanbul, Turkey.

- July 19 – August 3 – The 1980 Summer Olympics are held in Moscow, Soviet Union.
- July 25 – The album *Back in Black* is released by the Australian band AC/DC.
- July 27 – Mohammad Reza Pahlavi, deposed Shah of Iran, dies in Cairo.
- July 30
  - Vanuatu gains independence.
  - Israel's Knesset passes the Jerusalem Law.

August

- August 2 – A terrorist bombing at the railway station in Bologna, Italy kills 85 people and wounds more than 200.
- August 2 – Moscow Olympic Games football final: Czechoslovakia - GDR

Moscow Olympic Games on August 2, 1980

- August 7–31 – Lech Wałęsa leads the first of many strikes at the Gdańsk Shipyard.
- August 10 – Hurricane Allen (category 3) pounds southeastern Texas.
- August 14 – U.S. President Jimmy Carter defeats Senator Edward Kennedy to win renomination, at the 1980 Democratic National Convention in New York City.

- August 14 – Dorothy Stratten, the 1980 Playboy Playmate of the Year is murdered by estranged husband Paul Leslie Snider, who subsequently commits suicide.
- August 17 – In Australia, baby Azaria Chamberlain disappears from a campsite at Ayers Rock (Uluru), reportedly taken by a dingo.
- August 19 – In one of aviation's worst disasters, 301 people are killed when Saudia Flight 163 catches fire in Riyadh, Saudi Arabia.
- August 31 – Victory of the strike in Gdańsk Shipyard, Poland. The Gdańsk Agreement is signed, opening a way to start the first in the communist bloc free organization (not controlled by regime) "Solidarność" i.e. Solidarity.

September

- September 1 – Terry Fox is forced to end his Marathon of Hope run outside of Thunder Bay, Ontario, after finding out that the cancer has spread to his lungs.
- September 2 – Ford Europe launches the Escort MK3, a new front-wheel drive hatchback.
- September 3 – Zimbabwe breaks diplomatic and consular relations with South Africa, even though it maintains a commercial mission in Johannesburg.
- September 5 – The St. Gotthard Tunnel opens in Switzerland as the world's longest highway tunnel at 10.14 miles (16.32 km), stretching from Göschenen to Airolo.
- September 12 – Kenan Evren stages a military coup in Turkey. It stops political gang violence, but begins stronger

state violence leading to the execution of many young activists.

- September 17
  - After weeks of strikes at the Lenin Shipyard in Gdańsk, Poland, the nationwide independent trade union Solidarity is established.
  - Former Nicaraguan President Anastasio Somoza Debayle is killed in Asunción, Paraguay.
- September 21 – Bülent Ulusu, ex admiral, forms the new government of Turkey (44th government, composed mostly of technocrats).
- September 22
  - The command council of Iraq orders its army to "deliver its fatal blow on Iranian military targets," initiating the Iran–Iraq War.
  - Youth riots in Tallinn, the capital of the Estonian SSR, are quickly put down. Similar riots are organized on 1 October.
- September 26
  - 13 people are killed and 211 injured in the Oktoberfest terror attack.
  - The Mariel boatlift officially ends.
- September 27 – The Richmond Football Club defeats Collingwood by 81 points in the VFL Grand Final (They have yet to win another premiership since).
- September 29 – The *Washington Post* publishes Janet Cooke's story of Jimmy, an 8-year-old heroin addict (later proven to be fabricated).
- September 30 – Digital Equipment Corporation, Intel and Xerox introduce the DIX standard for Ethernet, which is the

first implementation outside of Xerox, and the first to support 10 Mbit/s speeds.

October

- October 1
  - Associated Newspapers announces that *The Evening News* will close and merge with the *Evening Standard*.
- October 3
  - The Police release their third studio album, *Zenyattà Mondatta*.
  - The main-belt asteroid 2404 Antarctica is discovered by Antonín Mrkos at Kleť, South Bohemian Region, Czechoslovakia.
- October 5 – British Leyland launches its new Metro, a three-door entry-level hatchback which is designed as the eventual replacement for the Mini. It gives BL a long-awaited modern competitor for the likes of the Ford Fiesta and Vauxhall Chevette.
- October 10
  - The 7.1 Mw El Asnam earthquake shakes northern Algeria with a maximum Mercalli intensity of X (*Extreme*), killing 2,633–5,000, and injuring 8,369–9,000.
  - British Prime Minister Margaret Thatcher delivers her famous "The lady's not for turning" speech.
- October 14 – The Staggers Rail Act is enacted, deregulating American railroads.
- October 15
  - James Callaghan announces his resignation as leader of the British Labour Party.

- James Hoskins forces his way into WCPO's television studio in Cincinnati, holding 9 employees hostage for several hours before releasing them and taking his own life.
- October 18 – The Fraser Government is re-elected for a third consecutive term in Australia with a reduced majority.
- October 20 – In continuous production since 1962, the last MGB roadster rolls off the assembly line at the Abingdon factory, ending production for the MG marque.
- October 21 – In Major League Baseball, The Philadelphia Phillies of the National League defeat the Kansas City Royals of the American League 4-1 in Game Six of the World Series to win the championship.
- October 22 – The Thomson Corporation says that *The Times* and all associated supplements will close in March 1981 if no buyer can be found.
- October 25 – Proceedings on the Hague Convention on the Civil Aspects of International Child Abduction conclude at The Hague.
- October 27 – Six Provisional Irish Republican Army prisoners in Maze prison refuse food and demand status as political prisoners; the hunger strike lasts until December.
- October 30
  - El Salvador and Honduras sign a peace treaty to put the border dispute fought over in 1969's Football War before the International Court of Justice.
  - Costa Rica recognizes the Sahrawi Arab Democratic Republic (SADR).
- October 31
  - The Polish government recognizes Solidarity.

- Reza Pahlavi, eldest son of the Shah of Iran, proclaims himself the rightful successor to the Peacock Throne.

November

- November – Duration of the CESDAP plan is extended indefinitely.
- November 4 – United States presidential election, 1980: Republican challenger and former Governor Ronald Reagan of California defeats incumbent Democratic President Jimmy Carter, exactly 1 year after the beginning of the Iran hostage crisis.
- November 10 – November 12 – Voyager program: The NASA space probe *Voyager I* makes its closest approach to Saturn, when it flies within 77,000 miles of the planet's cloud-tops and sends the first high resolution images of the world back to scientists on Earth.
- November 20
  - The Gang of Four trial begins in China.
  - A Texaco oil rig breaks through to a mine under Lake Peigneur.
- November 21
  - A fire at the MGM Grand Hotel and Casino on the Las Vegas Strip kills 85 people.
  - A then-record number of viewers (for an entertainment program) tune into the U.S. soap opera *Dallas* to learn who shot lead character J. R. Ewing. The "Who shot J.R.?" event is an international obsession.

- November 23 – The 6.9 Mw Irpinia earthquake shakes southern Italy with a maximum Mercalli intensity of X (*Extreme*), killing 2,483–4,900, and injuring 7,700–8,934.
- November 27 – Vanuatu recognizes the Sahrawi Arab Democratic Republic (SADR).

December

December 8: Former Beatles member John Lennon is shot dead outside his home in New York.

- December 2 – American missionary Jean Donovan and three Roman Catholic nuns are murdered by a military death squad in El Salvador while volunteering to do charity work during the country's civil war.
- December 4 – Led Zeppelin issue a press release announcing their break-up due to the death of their drummer John Bonham.
- December 8 – John Lennon is shot dead outside his apartment in New York City by Mark David Chapman.
- December 11 – CERCLA is enacted by the U.S. Congress.

- December 14 – Four people are murdered at Bob's Big Boy on La Cienega Boulevard in Los Angeles and 4 others are injured by two armed robbers, in what is one of the city's most brutal crimes ever.
- December 15 – The Academia de la Llingua Asturiana (Academy of the Asturian language) is created.
- December 16 – During a summit on the island of Bali, OPEC decides to raise the price of petroleum by 10%.

Date unknown

- The Right Livelihood Award is founded by Jakob von Uexkull. Hassan Fathy and Plenty International / Stephen Gaskin are its first winners.
- The World Hockey Association and NHL merge, adding teams in Connecticut, Quebec City, Alberta, and Manitoba to the league.
  - Accompanying the newly added Edmonton Oilers as the first team in Alberta, the Atlanta Flames move to Calgary.

Births

January

Zooey Deschanel

Jason Segel

Xavi

Marat Safin

- January 1
    - Richie Faulkner, British rock guitarist (Judas Priest)
    - Mark Nichols, Canadian curler
    - Elin Nordegren, Swedish model
- January 8
    - Adam Goodes, Australian rules footballer
    - Rachel Nichols, American actress
- January 9 – Sergio García, Spanish golfer
- January 10 – Sarah Shahi, American actress of Iranian and Spanish descent
- January 11 – Lovieanne Jung, American softball player
- January 12 – Ameriie, American singer
- January 13 – LaKisha Jones, American singer
- January 14
    - Ossama Haidar, Lebanese footballer
    - Hiroshi Tamaki, Japanese actor, model, and singer
    - Cory Gibbs, American footballer
    - Monika Kuszyńska, Polish singer and songwriter
    - Sosuke Sumitani, Japanese announcer
    - Yūko Kaida, Japanese voice actress

- January 16
  - Albert Pujols, Dominican Major League Baseball player
  - Michelle Wild, Hungarian actress
- January 17
  - Maksim Chmerkovskiy, Ukrainian dance champion, choreographer, and instructor
  - Zooey Deschanel, American actress
- January 18
  - Julius Peppers, American football player
  - Jason Segel, American actor
- January 19
  - Arvydas Macijauskas, Lithuanian basketball player
  - Jenson Button, British racecar driver
- January 20
  - Philippe Cousteau, Jr., American-French oceanographer
  - Philippe Gagnon, Canadian Paralympic swimmer
  - Kim Jeong-hoon, South Korean singer and actor
  - Brigitte Olivier, Belgian martial artist
  - Petra Rampre, Slovenian tennis player
  - Matthew Tuck, Welsh singer and guitarist (Bullet for My Valentine)
- January 21
  - Nana Mizuki, Japanese voice actress and singer
  - Kevin McKenna, Canadian footballer
- January 22
  - Jake Grove, American football player
  - Christopher Masterson, American actor
  - Adam Tuominen, Australian actor
- January 24
  - Nyncke Beekhuyzen, Dutch actress

- o Suzy, Portuguese singer
- January 25
  - o Christian Olsson, Swedish athlete
  - o Xavi, Spanish footballer
  - o Michelle McCool, American professional wrestler
- January 26 – Sanae Kobayashi, Japanese voice actress
- January 27 – Marat Safin, Russian tennis player
- January 28 – Nick Carter, American pop singer (Backstreet Boys)
- January 29
  - o Yael Bar Zohar, Israeli actress and model
  - o Jason James Richter, American actor
- January 30 – Wilmer Valderrama, Venezuelan/Colombian-American comedian
- January 31 – K.Maro, Canadian singer-songwriter

February

Christina Ricci

Chelsea Clinton

Jigme Khesar Namgyel Wangchuck

- February 2
  - Zhang Jingchu, Chinese actress
  - Gucci Mane, American rapper (birthname Radric Davis)
  - Nina Zilli, Italian singer-songwriter
- February 5
  - Jo Swinson, British MP
  - Robin Vik, Czech tennis player
  - Paul DelVecchio, American reality show personality
- February 6

- o Kim Poirier, Canadian actress
- o Luke Ravenstahl, American mayor of Pittsburgh
- o Mamiko Noto, Japanese voice actress
- February 8 – Yang Wei, Chinese gymnast
- February 10
  - o César Izturis, Venezuelan Major League Baseball player
  - o Steve Tully, English footballer
- February 11 – Matthew Lawrence, American actor (Boy Meets World)
- February 12
  - o Juan Carlos Ferrero, Spanish tennis player
  - o Christina Ricci, American actress
- February 14 – Michelle Ye, Hong Kong actress
- February 15
  - o Conor Oberst, American singer/songwriter
  - o Petr Elfimov, Belarusian singer
- February 16 – Ashley Lelie, American football player
- February 17
  - o Jason Ritter, American actor
  - o Vahe Tilbian, Ethiopian singer of Armenian descent
- February 18
  - o Cezar, Romanian opera singer and pianist
  - o Regina Spektor, Russian-American singer-songwriter
- February 19
  - o Mike Miller, American basketball player
  - o Ma Lin, Chinese table-tennis player
- February 20
  - o Imanol Harinordoquy, French rugby player
  - o Artur Boruc, Polish football (soccer) goalkeeper
  - o Yuichi Nakamura, Japanese voice actor

- February 21
  - Brad Fast, Canadian ice hockey player
  - Jigme Khesar Namgyel Wangchuck, King of Bhutan
- February 24 – Emma Johnson, Australian swimmer
- February 25 – Chris and Christy Knowings, American actors
- February 26 – Júlio César da Silva e Souza, Brazilian footballer
- February 27 – Chelsea Clinton, daughter of former U.S. President Bill Clinton and U.S. Secretary of State Hillary Clinton
- February 28
  - Tayshaun Prince, American basketball player
  - Piotr Giza, Polish footballer
- February 29
  - Simon Gagné, Canadian hockey player
  - Peter Scanavino, American actor

March

Laura Prepon

Ronaldinho

- March 1 – Shahid Afridi, Pakistani cricketer
- March 2
  - Chris Barker, English footballer
  - Lance Cade, American professional wrestler (d. 2010)
- March 4
  - Jung Da-bin, Korean actress (d. 2007)
  - Omar Bravo, Mexican footballer
  - Jack Hannahan, American baseball infielder
- March 5 – Jessica Boehrs, German singer and actress
- March 7 – Laura Prepon, American actress
- March 9 – Matthew Gray Gubler, American actor and director.
- March 11 – Gabriela Pichler, Swedish film director and screenwriter
- March 13 – Caron Butler, American basketball player
- March 14 – Aaron Brown, English footballer
- March 16 – Todd Heap, American football player
- March 17 – Katie Morgan, American porn actress and radio host

- March 18 – Alexei Yagudin, Russian figure skater
- March 19
  - Agnes Pihlava, Finnish pop singer
  - Johan Olsson, Swedish cross country skier
- March 20
  - Jamal Crawford, American basketball player
  - Hamada Helal, Egyptian singer
- March 21
  - Marit Bjørgen, Norwegian cross-country skier
  - Ronaldinho, Brazilian footballer
  - Deryck Whibley, Canadian singer, songwriter, and musician (Sum 41)
- March 23 – Russell Howard, English comedian
- March 29 – Andy Scott-Lee, British singer (3SL)
- March 30 – Yalın, Turkish pop singer and songwriter
- March 31
  - Chien-Ming Wang, Taiwanese Major League Baseball player
  - Maaya Sakamoto, Japanese voice actress, actress and singer

April

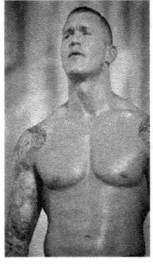

Randy Orton

Charlie Hunnam

Channing Tatum

Waylon

- April 1
  - Bijou Phillips, American actress and socialite
  - Randy Orton, American professional wrestler
  - Yūko Takeuchi, Japanese actress
- April 4 – Björn Wirdheim, Swedish race car driver

- April 8 – Ben Freeman, British actor
- April 9
  - Rachel Specter, American actress
  - Arlen Escarpeta, Belizean actor
- April 10
  - Sean Avery, Canadian ice hockey player
  - Kasey Kahne, American race car driver
  - Charlie Hunnam, English actor
- April 11 – Mark Teixeira, American baseball player
- April 12 – Brian McFadden, Irish rock singer (Westlife)
- April 13
  - Colleen Clinkenbeard, American voice actress
  - Kelli Giddish, American actress
- April 14 – Ayumi Ito, Japanese actress
- April 15 – Natalie Casey, English actress
- April 16
  - Samir Javadzadeh, Azerbaijani singer
  - Paul London, American professional wrestler
- April 17
  - Brenda Villa, American water polo player
  - Lee Hyun-il, South Korean badminton player
  - Alaina Huffman, Canadian film and television actress
- April 18 – Justin Amash, U.S. Representative
- April 20
  - Jasmin Wagner, German singer
  - Waylon, Dutch singer, member of The Common Linnets, Eurovision Song Contest 2014 runner-up
- April 21
  - Tony Romo, American football player
  - Vincent Lecavalier, Canadian hockey player

- April 22 – Nicolas Douchez, French footballer
- April 24
  - Austin Nichols, American actor
  - Karen Asrian, Armenian chess Grandmaster (d. 2008)
- April 25
  - Lee Spick, English snooker player (d. 2015)
  - Kazuhito Tadano, Japanese baseball player
- April 26
  - Jordana Brewster, American actress
  - Marlon King, Jamaican footballer
  - Channing Tatum, American actor and model
- April 27 – Zayed Khan, Indian actor
- April 28 – Josh Howard, American basketball player
- April 29 – Kian Egan, Irish singer (Westlife)
- April 30 – Luis Scola, Argentine basketball player

May

Ellie Kemper

Gotye

Steven Gerrard

- May 1 – Ana Claudia Talancón, Mexican actress
- May 2
    - Tim Borowski, German footballer
    - Ellie Kemper, American actress
    - Zat Knight, English footballer
- May 3 – Marcel Vigneron, American chef
- May 5
    - Maia Hirasawa, Swedish pop singer
    - Yossi Benayoun, Israeli footballer
- May 6
    - Taebin, Korean hip-hop artist (1TYM)
    - Kelly van der Veer, Dutch reality TV star

- Dimitris Diamantidis, Greek basketball player
- May 7 – Johan Kenkhuis, Dutch swimmer
- May 8 – Benny Yau, Canadian entertainer
- May 9
  - Grant Hackett, Australian swimmer
  - Carolin Kebekus, German comedian and actress
  - Norihiro Nishi, Japanese footballer
- May 10 – Pete Gray, Australian environmental activist (d. 2011)
- May 15 – Josh Beckett, American baseball player
- May 18 – Ali Zafar, Pakistani music composer, singer-songwriter, painter and actor
- May 19 – Dean Heffernan, Australian footballer
- May 21 – Gotye, Belgian-Australian multi-instrumentalist and singer-songwriter
- May 22 – Lucy Gordon, British actress (d. 2009)
- May 24 – Cecilia Cheung, Hong Kong actress
- May 28
  - Mark Feehily, Irish singer (Westlife)
  - Jørgen Strickert, Norwegian comedian
- May 29 – Michael Stasko, Canadian actor
- May 30 – Steven Gerrard, English footballer
- May 31 – Andy Hurley, American drummer (Fall Out Boy)

June

Venus Williams

Mike Fisher

Sarah Connor

- June 1
  - Oliver James, British actor
  - Damien Fahey, American MTV VJ, television host, and drummer
- June 2 – Lindsey Yamasaki, Japanese-American basketball player
- June 5 – Mike Fisher, Canadian hockey player
- June 7 – Henkka Seppälä, Finnish bassist (Children of Bodom)
- June 10
  - Francelino Matuzalem, Brazilian footballer
  - Wang Yuegu, Singaporean Olympic table tennis player

- June 13
  - Sarah Connor, German singer
  - Juan Carlos Navarro, Spanish basketball player
- June 15 – Almudena Cid Spanish rhythmic gymnast
- June 16
  - Brad Gushue, Canadian curler
  - Joey Yung, Hong Kong singer
- June 17
  - Kimeru, Japanese singer
  - Venus Williams, American tennis player
  - Jeph Jacques, American webcomic writer
- June 19 – Jason White, American football player
- June 22 – Ilya Bryzgalov, Russian ice hockey player
- June 23
  - Mark Greaney, Irish singer and guitarist (JJ72)
  - Ramnaresh Sarwan, West Indian cricketer
  - Manus Boonjumnong, Thai boxer
  - Francesca Schiavone, Italian tennis player
  - Jessica Taylor, English singer (Liberty X)
  - Pai Hsiao-yen, Taiwanese-Japanese murder victim (d.1997)
- June 24
  - Liane Balaban, Canadian actress
  - Minka Kelly, American actress
- June 25 – Nozomi Takeuchi, Japanese actress
- June 26
  - Michael Vick, American football player
  - Michael Jackson, English footballer
- June 29
  - Katherine Jenkins, Welsh soprano

- Martin Truex Jr, American race car driver

July

Olivia Munn

Eva Green

Jessica Simpson

Kristen Bell

- July 1
    - Patrick Aufiero, American ice hockey player
    - Nelson Cruz, Dominican baseball player
- July 3
    - Roland Mark Schoeman, South African swimmer
    - Olivia Munn, American actress and model
- July 4
    - Selma Bajrami, Bosnian turbo-folk singer
- July 5
    - Eva Green, French actress and model
    - Paul "DJ Pauly D" DelVecchio, American reality TV star
    - Jason Wade, American singer and guitarist (Lifehouse)
- July 6 – Pau Gasol, Spanish basketball player
- July 7 – Michelle Kwan, American figure skater
- July 8
    - Robbie Keane, Irish footballer
    - Yang Tae-Young, South Korean gymnast
- July 9 – Kathia Rodriguez, Puerto Rican actress
- July 10

- Adam Petty, American race car driver (d. 2000)
- Jessica Simpson, American singer
- James Rolfe, American director, actor and writer (on the Internet)
- July 15
  - Jasper Pääkkönen, Finnish actor and film producer
  - Reggie Abercrombie, American baseball player
  - JW-Jones, Canadian blues musician
- July 16
  - Adam Scott, Australian golfer
  - Svetlana Feofanova, Russian pole-vaulter
- July 17 – Ryan Miller, American ice hockey goaltender
- July 18 – Kristen Bell, American actress
- July 19
  - Mark Webber, American actor
  - Michelle Heaton, English singer (Liberty X)
- July 20 – Gisele Bündchen, Brazilian supermodel
- July 21 – CC Sabathia, American baseball player
- July 22
  - Dirk Kuyt, Dutch footballer
  - Kate Ryan, Belgian singer
- July 23 – Michelle Williams, American singer, actress, (Destiny's Child)
- July 25 – Rebeka Dremelj, Slovenian singer
- July 27 – Nick Nemeth, American professional wrestler
- July 28 – Noel Sullivan, Welsh singer (Hear'Say) and actor
- July 29 – Fernando González, Chilean tennis player
- July 30 – Diam's, French rapper

August

Macaulay Culkin

Chris Pine

William Levy

- August 3
  - Nadia Ali, Pakistani-American singer-songwriter

- o Dominic Moore, Canadian ice hockey player
- August 5 – Wayne Bridge, English footballer
- August 6 – Wilber Pan, American-Taiwanese singer-songwriter and actor
- August 8 – Craig Breslow, American baseball pitcher
- August 9
  - o Charlie David, Canadian actor
  - o Dominic Tabuna, Nauruan politician
- August 10 – Pua Magasiva, Samoan actor
- August 11 – Monika Pyrek, Polish pole vaulter
- August 12 – Maggie Lawson, American actress
- August 14 – Roy Williams, American football player
- August 16
  - o Julien Absalon, French mountain biker
  - o Vanessa Carlton, American singer
- August 17
  - o David Legwand, American ice hockey player
  - o Lene Marlin, Norwegian singer and musician
- August 18 – Damion Stewart, Jamaican footballer
- August 19
  - o Darius Campbell, Scottish singer-songwriter (aka Darius Danesh or Darius)
  - o Adrian Lulgjuraj, Albanian singer
- August 21
  - o Jon Lajoie, Canadian comedian
  - o Paul Menard, American race car driver
- August 23 – Rex Grossman, American football player
- August 24 – Rachael Carpani, Australian actress
- August 26
  - o Macaulay Culkin, American actor

- Chris Pine, American actor
- August 27 – Derrick Strait, American football player
- August 28 – Debra Lafave, American teacher
- August 29
  - William Levy, Cuban-American actor
  - David West, American basketball player

September

Michelle Williams

Yao Ming

Nigar Jamal

Ben Savage

Zachary Levi

- September 2 – Dany Sabourin, French Canadian ice hockey goaltender
- September 3
    - Jennie Finch, American softball player
    - Polina Smolova, Belarusian singer
- September 5 – Kevin Simm, English singer (Liberty X)
- September 6
    - Kerry Katona, English TV presenter and former pop star (Atomic Kitten)
    - Samuel Peter, Nigerian boxer and heavyweight champion
    - Joseph Yobo, Nigerian footballer
- September 7
    - Nigar Jamal, Azerbaijani singer, Eurovision Song Contest 2011 winner
    - Gabriel Milito, Argentine footballer
    - Mark Prior, American baseball player
- September 8 – Eric Hutchinson, American singer-songwriter
    - Neferteri Shepherd, African-American model and actress
- September 9
    - Denise Quiñones, Puerto Rican actress, Miss Universe 2001
    - Michelle Williams, American actress
- September 11 – Mike Comrie, Canadian ice hockey player
- September 12
    - Sean Burroughs, American baseball player
    - Yao Ming, Chinese basketball player
- September 13
    - Ben Savage, American actor (Boy Meets World)

- o Daisuke Matsuzaka, Japanese baseball player
- September 15 – Jolin Tsai, Taiwanese singer
- September 21
  - o Kareena Kapoor, Indian actress
  - o Autumn Reeser, American actress
- September 23
  - o Syu, Japanese guitarist
  - o Hooligan, Maltese rapper
- September 24
  - o Victoria Pendleton, English cyclist
  - o Amy-Joyce Hastings, Irish actress
- September 25 – T.I., African-American rap artist, film and music producer, actor and author
- September 26 – Daniel and Henrik Sedin, Swedish ice hockey players
- September 29
  - o Patrick Agyemang, Ghanaian footballer
  - o Dallas Green, musician (Alexisonfire, City and Colour)
  - o Zachary Levi, American actor
- September 30
  - o Martina Hingis, Swiss tennis player
  - o Emily Kokal, vocalist/guitarist of all-girl band Warpaint
  - o Guillermo Rigondeaux, Cuban boxer
  - o Arisa Ogasawara, Japanese voice actress

October

Nick Cannon

Kim Kardashian

Ben Foster

- October 4
  - Tomáš Rosický, Czech footballer
  - Me'Lisa Barber, American athlete
- October 5
  - James Toseland, English motorcycle racer
  - Ti West, American film director.
- October 8
  - Michael Mizanin, American professional wrestler
  - Nick Cannon, African-American actor, comedian, rapper, entrepreneur, record producer, radio, and television personality
- October 10
  - Sherine, Egyptian singer
  - Lynn Hung, Hong Kong actress
- October 12
  - Ledley King, English footballer
  - Nadzeya Ostapchuk, Belarusian athlete
- October 13
  - Ashanti, African-American singer
  - Scott Parker, English footballer
- October 14
  - Terrence McGee, American football player
  - Ben Whishaw, English actor
- October 15 – Tom Boonen, Belgian cyclist
- October 16
  - Sue Bird, American basketball player
  - Timana Tahu, Australian Rugby League player
- October 17 – Yekaterina Gamova, Russian volleyball player
- October 18 – Reetinder Singh Sodhi, Indian cricket player
- October 19 – José Bautista, Dominican baseball player

- October 21 – Kim Kardashian, American socialite and television personality
- October 24
  - Monica Arnold, African-American singer
  - Casey Wilson, American actress and comedian
- October 28
  - Alan Smith, English footballer
  - Christy Hemme, American professional wrestler
- October 29 – Ben Foster, American actor

November

Ryan Gosling

Monique Coleman

Nick Swisher

- November 4 – Sabrina Colie, Jamaican actress
- November 5
    - Christoph Metzelder, German footballer
    - Essaï Altounian, French-Armenian singer, songwriter, keyboardist, music producer and an actor
- November 6 – Anri Jokhadze, Georgian pop singer
- November 7 – Gervasio Deferr, Spanish gymnast
- November 10 – Calvin Chen, Taiwanese pop singer
- November 11 – Willie Parker, American football player
- November 12 – Ryan Gosling, Canadian actor
- November 13 – Monique Coleman, American actress
- November 15 – Kevin Staut, French equestrian
- November 16 – Kayte Christensen, American basketball player
- November 17 – Isaac Hanson, American musician
- November 18
    - Denny Hamlin, American race car driver
    - Dustin Kensrue, Canadian singer
    - François Duval, Belgian rally driver
    - Junichi Okada, Japanese singer
    - Luke Chadwick, English footballer
    - Mathew Baynton, English actor and writer

- o Minori Chihara, Japanese voice actress and singer
- November 19 – Adele Silva, English actress and model
- November 21
  - o Hank Blalock, American baseball player
  - o Hiroyuki Tomita, Japanese gymnast
  - o Elaine Yiu, Hong Kong actress
- November 22 – David Artell, English footballer
- November 23 – Jonathan Papelbon, American baseball player
- November 25
  - o John-Michael Liles, American hockey player
  - o Nick Swisher, American baseball player
- November 26 – Satoshi Ohno, Japanese singer
- November 28 – Lisa Middelhauve, German singer (Xandria)
- November 29 – Janina Gavankar, American actress and musician

December

Christina Aguilera

Jake Gyllenhaal

Eliza Dushku

- December 1 – Joel A. Sutherland, Canadian author
- December 3
    - Anna Chlumsky, American actress
    - Jim Sorgi, American football player
- December 5
    - Ibrahim Maalouf, Lebanese-born French trumpeter
    - Shizuka Itō, Japanese actor
- December 6
    - Steve Lovell, English footballer
    - Kei Yasuda, Japanese singer

- December 7 – John Terry, English footballer
- December 9
  - Simon Helberg, American actor and comedian
  - Ryder Hesjedal, Canadian professional cyclist
- December 10
  - Marina Orlova, Internet celebrity
  - Sarah Chang, American violinist
- December 13
  - Satoshi Tsumabuki, Japanese actor
  - Bosco Wong, Hong Kong actor
- December 15
  - Neil McDermott, English actor
  - Sergio Pizzorno, English guitarist and songwriter (Kasabian)
- December 16 – Axle Whitehead, Australian actor, singer and songwriter and former Video Hits host
- December 18 – Christina Aguilera, American singer
- December 19 – Jake Gyllenhaal, American actor
- December 20
  - Ashley Cole, English footballer
  - Chris Edwards, English musician, member of alternative rock band Kasabian
  - Fitz Hall, English footballer
- December 22 – Chris Carmack, American actor
- December 23 – Cody Ross, American baseball player
- December 25 – Laura Sadler, English actress (d. 2003)
- December 27 – Bernard Berrian, American football player
- December 30 – Eliza Dushku, American actress
- December 31 – Richie McCaw, New Zealand rugby player

Deaths

January

Jimmy Durante

- January 1 – Adolph Deutsch, American composer (b. 1897)
- January 3 – Joy Adamson, Austrian-born conservationist and author (b. 1910)
- January 7 – Simonne Mathieu, French tennis champion (b. 1908)
- January 8 – John Mauchly, American physicist and inventor (b. 1907)
- January 10
    - George Meany, American labor leader (b. 1894)
    - Bo Rein, American football coach (b. 1945)
- January 11 – Barbara Pym, English novelist (b. 1913)
- January 13 – Andre Kostelanetz, Russian-born conductor and arranger (b. 1901)
- January 17 – Barbara Britton, American actress (b. 1919)
- January 18 – Sir Cecil Beaton, English photographer (b. 1904)

- January 19 – William O. Douglas, American Supreme Court Justice (b. 1898)
- January 21 – Georges Painvin, French cryptographer (b. 1886)
- January 24 – Lil Dagover, German actress (b. 1887)
- January 27 – Eric Wyndham White, British administrator and economist, first Director-General of the GATT (b. 1913)
- January 28 – Franco Evangelisti, Italian composer (b. 1926)
- January 29 – Jimmy Durante, American actor, singer, and comedian (b. 1893)
- January 30 – Professor Longhair, American musician (b. 1918)
- January 31 – Eduardo Cáceres, former Vice President of Guatemala (b. 1906)

February

- February 2
  - Hanna Rovina, Russian-born Israeli actress (b. 1889)
  - William Howard Stein, American chemist, Nobel Prize laureate (b. 1911)
- February 6 – Albert Kotin, American abstract expressionist painter (b. 1907)
- February 7 – Richard Williams (RAAF officer), Royal Australian Air Force officer (b. 1890)
- February 8
  - Isadora Bennett, American publicity agent (b. 1900)
  - Nikos Xilouris, Greek pop singer (b. 1936)
- February 9 – Tom Macdonald, Welsh journalist and novelist (b. 1900)

- February 10 – Wels Eicke, Australian rules football player (b. 1893)
- February 12 – Muriel Rukeyser, American poet (b. 1913)
- February 13 – David Janssen, American actor (b. 1931)
- February 14 – Luitkonwar Rudra Baruah, Assamese composer and actor
- February 17
    - Jerry Fielding, American conductor and music director (b. 1922)
    - Graham Sutherland, English artist (b. 1903)
- February 18 – Gale Robbins, American singer and actress (b. 1921)
- February 19 – Bon Scott, Scottish-born Australian rock singer (AC/DC) (b. 1946)
- February 20
    - Joseph Banks Rhine, American parapsychologist (b. 1895)
    - Alice Longworth, U.S. President Theodore Roosevelt's daughter, wife of Nicholas Longworth (b. 1884)
- February 22 – Oskar Kokoschka, Austrian painter and poet (b. 1886)
- February 24 – Clement Martyn Doke, South African linguist (b. 1893)
- February 27
    - George Tobias, American actor (b. 1901)
    - Shin'ichi Hisamatsu, Japanese philosopher (b. 1889)
- February 28 – James Goff, American football & basketball head coach (b. 1912)
- February 29 – Gil Elvgren, American pin-up artist (b. 1914)

March

Óscar Romero

Jesse Owens

- March 1
    - Dixie Dean, English football player (b. 1907)
    - Wilhelmina, Dutch-born American high-fashion model and owner of model agency (b. 1940)
    - Daniil Khrabrovitsky, Soviet film director (b. 1923)
- March 5
    - Jay Silverheels, Native American actor (b. 1912)
    - Winifred Wagner, German daughter-in-law of Richard Wagner, close friend of Adolf Hitler (b. 1897)
- March 9 – Heinz Linge, Hitler's personal valet (b. 1913).

- March 10 – Herman Tarnower, American doctor and murder victim (b. 1910)
- March 11 – Maud Hart Lovelace, American author (b. 1892)
- March 13 – Roland Symonette, 1st Premier of the Bahamas (b. 1898)
- March 14
  - Anna Jantar, Polish singer (b. 1950)
  - Mohammad Hatta, Indonesia's first vice president (b. 1902)
  - Félix Rodríguez de la Fuente, Spanish naturalist and television presenter (b. 1928)
- March 18
  - Jessica Dragonette, American singer (b. 1900)
  - Erich Fromm, German-born psychologist and philosopher (b. 1900)
  - Louise Lovely, Australian actress (b. 1895)
  - Tamara de Lempicka, Polish-born painter (b. 1898)
- March 21 – Peter Stoner, American mathematician, astronomer and Christian apologist (b. 1888)
- March 24
  - John Barrie, British actor (b. 1917)
  - Pierre Etchebaster, French real tennis player (b. 1893)
  - Óscar Romero, El Salvador Roman Catholic archbishop (assassinated) (b. 1917)
- March 25
  - Roland Barthes, French literary critic and writer (b. 1915)
  - Walter Susskind, Czech conductor (b. 1913)
  - James Wright, American poet (b. 1927)
  - Milton H. Erickson, American psychiatrist (b.1901)

- March 28 – Dick Haymes, Argentine actor and singer (b. 1916)
- March 29 – Mantovani, Italian-born conductor and arranger (b. 1905)
- March 31
  - Vladimír Holan, Czech poet (b. 1905)
  - Jesse Owens, African-American athlete (b. 1913)

April

Jean-Paul Sartre

Alfred Hitchcock

- April 2 – Stanley Forman Reed, American Supreme Court Justice (b. 1884)
- April 4 – Red Sovine, American country and folk singer-songwriter (b. 1917)
- April 6 – John Collier, English writer (b. 1901)
- April 10 – Kay Medford, American actress (b. 1914)

- April 11 – Ümit Kaftancıoğlu, Turkish writer (b. 1935)
- April 12 – Clark McConachy, New Zealand snooker and billiards player (b. 1895)
- April 13 – Karl Stegger, Danish actor (b. 1913)
- April 15
  - Raymond Bailey, American actor (b. 1904)
  - Marshall Reed, American film and television actor (b. 1917)
  - Jean-Paul Sartre, French philosopher and writer, Nobel Prize laureate (b. 1905)
- April 19 – Tony Beckley, English character actor (b. 1927)
- April 20 –
  - Katherine Kennicott Davis, American composer (b. 1892)
  - Helmut Käutner, German director (b. 1908)
- April 21 – Sohrab Sepehri, Persian poet and painter (b. 1928)
- April 22
  - Jane Froman, American singer and actress (b. 1907)
  - Fritz Strassmann, German chemist (b. 1902)
- April 24 – Alejo Carpentier, Cuban writer (b. 1904)
- April 25 – Mario Bava, Italian film director (b. 1914)
- April 26 – Cicely Courtneidge, British actress (b. 1893)
- April 27 – John Culshaw, British recording producer and musicologist (b. 1924)
- April 28 – Thomas G. W. Settle, American record-setting balloonist and admiral (b. 1895)
- April 29 – Alfred Hitchcock, British suspense film director (b. 1899)
- April 30 – Luis Muñoz Marín, Puerto Rican poet, journalist, and politician (b. 1898)

May

Josip Broz Tito

- May 2 – George Pal, Hungarian-born animator and producer (b. 1904)
- May 4
    - Kay Hammond, English actress (b. 1909)
    - Josip Broz Tito, President of Yugoslavia (b. 1892)
- May 5 – Isabel Briggs Myers, American psychological theorist and co-creator of the Myers-Briggs Type Indicator (b. 1897)
- May 8 – Geoffrey Baker, English field marshal (b. 1912)
- May 12 – Lillian Roth, American actress (b. 1910)
- May 14
    - Carl Ebert, German theatre and opera director (b. 1887)
    - Hugh Griffith, Welsh actor (b. 1912)
- May 16 – Marin Preda, Romanian writer (b. 1922)
- May 18
    - David A. Johnston, American volcanologist (b. 1949) (killed by eruption of Mount St. Helens))
    - Ian Curtis, British musician and singer (Joy Division) (b. 1956)

- May 21 – Ida Kamińska, Polish actress (b. 1899)
- May 28 – Rolf Nevanlinna, Finnish mathematician (b. 1895)

June

- June 1 – Rube Marquard, American baseball player (New York Giants) and a member of the MLB Hall of Fame (b. 1886)
- June 7
  - Henry Miller, American writer (b. 1891)
  - Elizabeth Craig, British chef and writer (b. 1883)
  - Philip Guston, American painter (b. 1912)
- June 8 – Ernst Busch, German singer and actor (b. 1900)
- June 12
  - Masayoshi Ōhira, Prime Minister of Japan (b. 1910)
  - Billy Butlin, South African–born Canadian founder of Butlins Holiday Camps (b. 1899)
  - Milburn Stone, American actor (b. 1904)
- June 13 – Walter Rodney, Guyanese historian and political figure (b. 1942)
- June 20 – Amy Key Clarke, English mystical poet (b. 1892)
- June 21 – Bert Kaempfert, German orchestra leader and songwriter (b. 1923)
- June 23
  - Clyfford Still, American painter (b. 1904)
  - John Laurie, British actor (b. 1897)
  - Sanjay Gandhi, Indian son of Indira Gandhi (air crash) (b. 1946)
  - V. V. Giri, Indian politician and 4th President of India (b. 1894)

- June 24 – Boris Kaufman, Russian cinematographer (b. 1897)
- June 27 – Carey McWilliams, American author, editor, and lawyer (b. 1905)
- June 28 – José Iturbi, Spanish conductor and musician (b. 1895)

July

Peter Sellers

Shah Muhammad Reza Pahlavi

- July – Robert Brackman, American painter (b. 1898)
- July 1 – C. P. Snow, British physicist and novelist (b. 1905)

- July 4 – Gregory Bateson, British anthropologist, anthropologist, social scientist, linguist, semiotician and cyberneticist (b. 1904)
- July 6 – Gail Patrick, American actress (b. 1911)
- July 7
  - Reginald Gardiner, English actor (b. 1903)
  - Dore Schary, American film writer, director, and producer (b. 1905)
- July 9
  - Vinicius de Moraes, Brazilian writer, poet and diplomat (b. 1913)
  - Kate Molale, South African anti-Apartheid activist (b. 1928)
- July 15 – Ben Selvin, American orchestra leader and recording artist (b. 1898)
- July 17
  - Don "Red" Barry, American actor (b. 1912)
  - Boris Delaunay, Russian mathematician (b. 1890)
- July 23 – Keith Godchaux, American musician (The Grateful Dead) (b. 1948)
- July 24
  - Uttam Kumar (Arun Kumar Chatterjee), Bengali actor (b. 1926)
  - Peter Sellers, English comedian and actor (b. 1925)
- July 25 – Vladimir Vysotsky, Russian singer-songwriter, poet, actor (b. 1938)
- July 26
  - Allen Hoskins, American actor (b. 1920)
  - Kenneth Tynan, English theatre critic (b. 1927)
- July 27 – Mohammad Reza Pahlavi, Shah of Iran (b. 1919)

- July 31
  - Pascual Jordan, German physicist (b. 1902)
  - Mohammed Rafi, Indian singer (b. 1924)
  - Bobby Van, American actor (b. 1928)

August

- August 1
  - Patrick Depailler, French racing driver (b. 1944)
  - Strother Martin, American actor (b. 1919)
- August 2 – Donald Ogden Stewart, American writer (b. 1894)
- August 7 – Jackie Cochran, American pilot (b. 1906)
- August 9 – Elliott Nugent, American actor (b. 1896)
- August 10 – Yahya Khan, Pakistani general and statesman, 3rd President of Pakistan (b. 1917)
- August 14 – Dorothy Stratten, Canadian model (murdered) (b. 1960)
- August 15 – William Hood Simpson, American general (b. 1888)
- August 19 – Otto Frank, German father of Jewish diarist Anne Frank (b. 1889)
- August 20 – Joe Dassin, American-born French singer-songwriter (b. 1938)
- August 22 – Norman Shelley, British actor (b. 1903)
- August 24 – Yootha Joyce, British actress (b. 1927)
- August 25 – Gower Champion, American theatre director, choreographer, and dancer (b. 1919)
- August 26
  - Tex Avery, American cartoonist (b. 1908)

- Miliza Korjus, Estonian-Polish opera singer (b. 1909)

September

- September 3
  - Barbara O'Neil, American actress (b. 1909)
  - Dirch Passer, Danish actor (b. 1926)
  - Duncan Renaldo, American actor (b. 1904)
- September 8 – Willard Libby, American chemist, Nobel Prize laureate (b. 1908)
- September 12 – Lillian Randolph, American actress (b. 1898)
- September 15 – Bill Evans, American jazz pianist (b. 1929)
- September 16
  - Jean Piaget, Swiss psychologist (b. 1896)
  - Julio Franco Arango, Colombian Roman Catholic bishop (b. 1914)
- September 17 – Anastasio Somoza Debayle, former President of Nicaragua (b. 1925)
- September 18 – Katherine Anne Porter, American author (b. 1890)
- September 19 – Sol Lesser, American film producer (b. 1890)
- September 23 – Jacobus Johannes Fouché, 2nd State President of South Africa (b. 1898)
- September 25
  - John Bonham, British rock drummer (Led Zeppelin) (b. 1948)
  - Lewis Milestone, American film director (b. 1895)
  - Marie Under, Estonian poet (b. 1883)

October

- October 6 – Hattie Jacques, British actress (b. 1922)
- October 7 – Sydney Gordon Russell, English designer and craftsman (b. 1892)
- October 10 – Billie Thomas, American actor (*Buckwheat, Our Gang*) (b. 1931)
- October 20 – Lady Isobel Barnett, British television personality (b. 1918)
- October 21 – Hans Asperger, Austrian pediatrician after whom Asperger syndrome was named (b. 1906)
- October 25
  - Sahir Ludhianvi, Urdu/Hindustani poet and Hindi film lyricist (b. 1921)
  - Virgil Fox, American organist (b. 1912)
  - Víctor Galíndez, Argentine boxer (race car accident) (b. 1948)
- October 27
  - Steve Peregrin Took, British rock musician (T. Rex) (b. 1949)
  - John Hasbrouck Van Vleck, American physicist, Nobel Prize laureate (b. 1899)
- October 29 – Giorgio Borġ Olivier, 7th Prime Minister of Malta (b. 1911)

November

Steve McQueen

Mae West

- November 1
  - Walker County Jane Doe, unidentified murder victim (b. 1960-1966)
- November 4
  - Elsie MacGill, Canadian aeronautical engineer (b. 1904)
  - Johnny Owen, Welsh professional boxer (b. 1956)
- November 7 – Steve McQueen, American actor (b. 1930)
- November 9
  - Gloria Guinness, Mexican-born American fashion icon (b. 1912)

- ○ Carmel Myers, American actress (b. 1899)
- ○ Victor Sen Yung, American actor (b. 1915)
- November 16 – Boris Aronson, Russian set designer (b. 1898)
- November 18 – Conn Smythe, Canadian NHL coach (b. 1895)
- November 19 – E. J. Bowen, English chemist (b. 1898)
- November 20 – John McEwen, 18th Prime Minister of Australia (b. 1900)
- November 22
  - ○ Norah McGuinness, Northern Irish painter and illustrator (b. 1901)
  - ○ Mae West, American actress (b. 1893)
- November 24 – George Raft, American actor (b. 1895)
- November 26 – Rachel Roberts, British actress (b. 1927)
- November 27 – F. Burrall Hoffman, American architect (b. 1882)
- November 29
  - ○ Dorothy Day, American social progressive (b. 1897)
  - ○ Babe London, American actress and comedian (b. 1901)

December

John Lennon

Colonel Sanders

- December 2 – Romain Gary, Lithuanian-born writer (b. 1914)
- December 3 – Sir Oswald Mosley, British fascist leader (b. 1896)
- December 4
  - Francisco de Sá Carneiro, Prime Minister of Portugal (plane crash) (b. 1934)
  - Stanisława Walasiewicz, Polish-born runner (b. 1911)
- December 7 – Darby Crash, American rock songwriter, singer (Germs) (suicide) (b. 1958)
- December 8 – John Lennon, British singer, songwriter, and guitarist (The Beatles) (murdered) (b. 1940)
- December 12 – Erich Jantsch, Austrian astrophysicist (b. 1929)
- December 16
  - Colonel Sanders, American fast-food entrepreneur (b. 1890)
  - Hellmuth Walter, German engineer and inventor (b. 1900)
  - Peter Collinson, British film director (b. 1936)
- December 18

- o Alexei Kosygin, Russian politician, Premier of the Soviet Union (b. 1904)
- o Sir Albert Margai, second prime minister of Sierra Leone (b. 1910)
- o Enrique Hertzog, 49th President of Bolivia (b. 1896)
- December 19 – Héctor José Cámpora, Argentine Peronist politician, former president (b. 1909)
- December 21 – Marc Connelly, American playwright (b. 1890)
- December 23 – Frank Norman, English novelist, playwright and autobiographer (b. 1930)
- December 24
  - o Karl Dönitz, German admiral and briefly President of Germany (b. 1891)
  - o Siggie Nordstrom, American model, actress, entertainer, socialite and lead singer (The Nordstrom Sisters) (b. 1893)
- December 25 – Victoria Drummond, first woman marine engineer in Britain (b. 1894)
- December 26 – Richard Chase, American serial killer (b. 1950)
- December 28 – Sam Levene, American actor (b. 1905)
- December 29 – Tim Hardin, American musician (b. 1941)
- December 31
  - o Raoul Walsh, American film director (b. 1887)
  - o Marshall McLuhan, Canadian author and professor (b. 1911)

Nobel Prizes

- Physics – James Watson Cronin, Val Logsdon Fitch
- Chemistry – Paul Berg, Walter Gilbert, Frederick Sanger
- Medicine – Baruj Benacerraf, Jean Dausset, George D. Snell
- Literature – Czesław Miłosz
- Peace – Adolfo Pérez Esquivel
- Economics – Lawrence Klein

In the News.

Start of Iran -- Iraq War.

Ronald Reagan Elected President of the USA.

Terrorists seize Iran embassy and hostages in London leading to the British SAS storming embassy and releasing hostages.

US leads boycott of Moscow Olympics in protest at Soviet invasion of Afghanistan.

Mount St. Helens erupts on May 18th in Washington killing 57.

The Killer Clown (John Wayne Gacy Jr) sentenced to death for the murder of 33 boys and young men.

Former Beatle John Lennon is shot to death.

The Winter Olympic Games are held in Lake Placid, New York, United States.

Voyager 1 probe sends the first high resolution images of Saturn back to scientists and confirms the existence of Janus, a moon of Saturn.

Popular Films - Star Wars Episode V: The Empire Strikes Back, Superman II, Nine to Five, Raging Bull, Coal Miner's Daughter.

1980 Calender.

January 1980

Sun	Mon	Tue	Wed	Thu	Fri	Sat
		1	2	3	4	5
6	7	8	9	10	11	12
13	14	15	16	17	18	19
20	21	22	23	24	25	26
27	28	29	30	31		

February 1980

Sun	Mon	Tue	Wed	Thu	Fri	Sat
					1	2
3	4	5	6	7	8	9
10	11	12	13	14	15	16
17	18	19	20	21	22	23
24	25	26	27	28	29	

March 1980

Sun	Mon	Tue	Wed	Thu	Fri	Sat
						1
2	3	4	5	6	7	8
9	10	11	12	13	14	15
16	17	18	19	20	21	22
23	24	25	26	27	28	29
30	31					

April 1980

Sun	Mon	Tue	Wed	Thu	Fri	Sat
		1	2	3	4	5
6	7	8	9	10	11	12
13	14	15	16	17	18	19
20	21	22	23	24	25	26
27	28	29	30			

May 1980

Sun	Mon	Tue	Wed	Thu	Fri	Sat
				1	2	3
4	5	6	7	8	9	10
11	12	13	14	15	16	17
18	19	20	21	22	23	24
25	26	27	28	29	30	31

June 1980

Sun	Mon	Tue	Wed	Thu	Fri	Sat
1	2	3	4	5	6	7
8	9	10	11	12	13	14
15	16	17	18	19	20	21
22	23	24	25	26	27	28
29	30					

July 1980

Sun	Mon	Tue	Wed	Thu	Fri	Sat
		1	2	3	4	5
6	7	8	9	10	11	12
13	14	15	16	17	18	19
20	21	22	23	24	25	26
27	28	29	30	31		

August 1980

Sun	Mon	Tue	Wed	Thu	Fri	Sat
					1	2
3	4	5	6	7	8	9
10	11	12	13	14	15	16
17	18	19	20	21	22	23
24	25	26	27	28	29	30
31						

September 1980

Sun	Mon	Tue	Wed	Thu	Fri	Sat
	1	2	3	4	5	6
7	8	9	10	11	12	13
14	15	16	17	18	19	20
21	22	23	24	25	26	27
28	29	30				

October 1980

Sun	Mon	Tue	Wed	Thu	Fri	Sat
			1	2	3	4
5	6	7	8	9	10	11
12	13	14	15	16	17	18
19	20	21	22	23	24	25
26	27	28	29	30	31	

November 1980

Sun	Mon	Tue	Wed	Thu	Fri	Sat
						1
2	3	4	5	6	7	8
9	10	11	12	13	14	15
16	17	18	19	20	21	22
23	24	25	26	27	28	29
30						

December 1980

Sun	Mon	Tue	Wed	Thu	Fri	Sat
	1	2	3	4	5	6
7	8	9	10	11	12	13
14	15	16	17	18	19	20
21	22	23	24	25	26	27
28	29	30	31			

www.ingramcontent.com/pod-product-compliance
Lightning Source LLC
Chambersburg PA
CBHW072015290526
45787CB00013B/914